THWACKED!

A Fractured Tale of Frogs, Folks and Falling Skies

By Dave and Jean Perry

This symbol indicates a track number on the CD for the listening version of the song (includes vocals).

This symbol indicates a track number on the CD for the accompaniment version of the song (instruments only).

ISBN 978-1-4234-9856-8

Performance time: approximately 35 minutes

Shawnee Press

EXCLUSIVELY DISTRIBUTED BY

HAL•LEONARD®
CORPORATION

7777 W. BLUEMOUND RD. P.O. BOX 13819 MILWAUKEE, WI 53213

Continuing the Tradition of Shawnee Press Excellence

Visit Hal Leonard Online at
www.halleonard.com

Visit Shawnee Press Online at
www.shawneepress.com

CONTENTS
Scenes and Musical Numbers

CAST

Unless otherwise indicated, each character sings with the cast in three songs.

NARRATOR 1:	Boy or girl with good diction. Serious and straightforward.
NARRATOR 2:	Boy or girl with good diction. The comedy part of this narrator team.
FROG:	Boy or girl. Fairly serious and straightforward. Has a solo.
FROGGIE:	Girl with good diction. Has short solos.
FROGGER:	Boy who is a bit rough around the edges. Has short solos.
TINKER:	Handyman and salesman combined. Boy or girl. Has short solos.
ALEXIS:	A young girl. One of the three maids. Somewhat shy.
DENISE:	A young girl. One of the three maids. A connoisseur of fine food.
PRISCILLA:	A young girl. One of the three maids. Squeamish.
ED:	A student. Not afraid to speak out.
BECKA:	A student. Outspoken.
EMILY:	A student. Sympathetic.
MIKE:	A student. Always ready to spring into action.
RACHEL:	A student. Practical, logical, seeks the truth. Has a solo.
MISS FINKLETON:	The Librarian; prim and proper. Has a solo.
COACH KLAXTON:	The Physical Education Teacher; rough and ready. Has a solo.
MAYOR:	Somewhat pompous; enjoys attention. Boy or girl. If girl, then the song, "He Will Save the Day!" should be changed to "She Will Save the Day!"; with gender changes in the lyrics and also in the dialogue wherever the *Mayor is mentioned. Has a solo.
COUNCIL MEMBER #1:	No leadership; questions everything. Boy or girl. Sings.
COUNCIL MEMBER #2:	Nervous and timid. Boy or girl. Sings.
COUNCIL MEMBER #3:	Usually responds with the same words. Boy or girl. Sings.
COUNCIL MEMBER #4:	Thoughtful, a person of few words or opinions. Boy or girl. Sings.
PRINCE:	May double as a member of the chorus until the final scene.
TOWNSPEOPLE:	Children and adults. Sing.

*Suggestions: Madame Mayor, Miss Mayor

STAGE SETTING

Two sets are needed. These may be in separate units to be moved on and off center stage, or they may remain in place throughout the show. This could be done with the school gym taking up the majority of the left and center stage, and the log and tree being placed at stage right, possibly on side steps or in front of the stage. Your performance area will dictate how you handle this, but basically, it is your decision to do what works best for you.

Set #1: The **Swamp** will have a tree, some shrubbery, and a log for the three frogs to sit on.

Set #2: The **School**, located left and center stage, should be an open space with a backdrop that gives the appearance of a school hop.

COSTUMES

This musical takes place in a fairy tale setting. Your costuming should aim in that direction. The frogs should be dressed in green. Tinker should wear a coat, as colorful as possible, with an assortment of trinkets and ribbons hanging from it. The maids could be dressed in identical outfits, perhaps each a different pastel color. Miss Finkleton is a librarian. Coach Klaxton is the physical education teacher. Both should be dressed according to their area of expertise. The Mayor should wear a solid dark suit with a white shirt and a large red sash (worn diagonally from one shoulder to the waist). Village women should wear peasant blouses with full, long skirts. Village men would be fine in dark coats or colored shirts, suspenders, and black, dark blue, or tan pants. Girls should wear peasant blouses with full, knee-length skirts, and boys dressed in white, short-sleeved shirts with dark shorts and suspenders. All townspeople should wear dark shoes and the Council Members should be dressed the same. The Prince should have a small crown and typical prince clothing.

PROPS

- Tinker's sack full of junk, including pots, pans, and a hand mirror to give to the Prince
- a pad and pencil for Rachel to carry with her to take notes
- eyeglasses on a chain for Miss Finkleton to hang around her neck
- a ruler for Miss Finkleton to use
- a stack of books for Miss Finkleton to carry in
- a whistle for Coach Klaxton to wear on a lanyard around his neck
- a milk jug or pitcher for Alexis to carry
- a basket of eggs for Denise
- a basket of cheese for Priscilla
- a small crown for the Prince
- an oversized acorn (large enough for the audience to see)

STAGING SUGGESTIONS FOR SONGS

1. **Prologue** – *Cast*
Chorus enters from both sides in front of curtain and tells the story of how the Prince became a frog.

2. **Swamp Serenade** – *Frog*
As the music begins, the curtain opens to reveal Frog sitting on a log under a tree, looking around and enjoying the peaceful evening. Froggie and Frogger are sitting nearby, asleep.

3a. **It's Falling** – *Frog, Froggie, Frogger, and Tinker*
Frogs are telling Tinker about the sky falling. Tinker is initially skeptical but as the song progresses, he is swayed by their story and becomes convinced that the sky is falling.

3b. **It's Falling** – *Frog, Froggie, Frogger, Tinker, and Maids*
Similar to the previous song, the frogs and Tinker join forces to tell the maids about the sky falling. By the end of the song, the maids have also been swayed into believing that the sky is falling.

4. **The Hop** – *Students, Teachers, Townspeople, Tinker, Maids, and Frogs*
"The Hop" is a dance at the school. Dance movements can be taken from the lyrics (flap like a chicken – shuffle around like a chicken scratching; hop like a frog – jump up then down on both feet at the same time, etc.). When the frogs, maids, and Tinker enter, the Townspeople pull them into the dance.

5a. **We're Gonna Win!** – *Miss Finkleton, Coach Klaxton, Students, Townspeople, Tinker, Maids, and Frogs*
This is a rousing song that Coach Klaxton uses to build confidence and enthusiasm with Miss Finkleton and the Chorus. Think pep rally, marching band, pom-poms.

5b. **He Will Save the Day!** – *Students, Teachers, Townspeople, Tinker, Maids, Frogs*
With a certain amount of excitement and awe, the townspeople sing the virtues of their elected leader. If the Mayor is played by a girl, this should be changed to "She Will Save the Day."

6a. **It Wouldn't Be Wise** – *Mayor, Council, Students, Teachers, Townspeople, Tinker, Maids, and Frogs*
This song is actually a dialogue in which the Mayor explains why he needs to research the problem before arriving at a solution. The townspeople respond by telling him about the urgency of the problem. Toward the end, the Council Members support the Mayor in the debate.

6b. **It Wouldn't Be Wise** – *Instrumental*
Played while cast leaves stage, winds through audience, and returns to the swamp. The Narrators have some dialogue during this. You may wish to repeat the music and then fade once everyone is in place.

7. **Believe in Yourself** – *Rachel and Cast*
Rachel breaks away from Miss Finkleton's grasp and crosses SL, defeated and almost in tears. As the music begins, everyone remains frozen, but sings. As the chorus sings, Rachel looks around up in the air for the voices, but finally accepts it and sings her part.

8. **Amazing!** – *Cast*
The Prince tells his story about how and why he was turned into a frog. The entire cast responds in a chorus of amazement.

9. **Exit Music** – *Instrumental*
This may be played during bows and may also be used as the audience exits.

Narrators enter DSL in front of curtain. Narrator 1 carries a large book entitled "Thwacked!" Narrator 1 opens the book and reads …

NARRATOR 1:	Once upon a time …
NARRATOR 2:	*(interrupts … to audience)* Boy, do we have a story for you!
NARRATOR 1:	*(begins again)* As I was saying … once upon a time there was a King and a Queen and they lived in a castle.
NARRATOR 2:	Where else?
NARRATOR 1:	And they had a son who was spoiled and rude.
NARRATOR 2:	Not like me.
NARRATOR 1:	His bad behavior gave him a major problem.
NARRATOR 2:	Is this where I sing?
NARRATOR 1:	No.
NARRATOR 2:	You're gonna sing?
NARRATOR 1:	No. This is where the chorus sings.
NARRATOR 2:	Brilliant idea!

Chorus enters SR and SL in front of curtain. Narrators may exit SL or may stay and sing with the chorus.

1. PROLOGUE
All Except Frogs and Prince

By
DAVE *and* JEAN PERRY (ASCAP)

Continuing the Tradition of Shawnee Press Excellence

want - ed bugs and flies. He found that sit - ting on a log was

right where he should be; There, in the swamp, un - der - neath a big oak tree.

So there he sits now, all green and slim - y, by a

pond that he calls home. This is his sto - ry. It's quite a -

All exit SR and SL and Narrators return to their positions SL.

NARRATOR 1:   And so, as time passed, he settled into his life as a frog and forgot he'd ever been a Prince.

NARRATOR 2:   He whiled away his days sitting … *(stops, coughs, clears his throat)* Excuse me. I've got a frog in my throat. *(regains his composure)* He whiled away his days sitting on a log down in the swamp.

NARRATOR 1:   And in the evenings, an occasional song would come to his lips …

NARRATOR 2:   … making the other frogs green with envy.

NARRATOR 1:   *(disgusted … to Narrator 2)* Do you mind? I'm trying to set the mood.

NARRATOR 2:   Right! I'll just hop along. *(chuckles to himself)*

Both Narrators exit SL as the music begins and curtain opens to reveal one frog sitting under a tree on a log, DSR. Two other frogs are sleeping nearby.

2. SWAMP SERENADE
Frog

By
DAVE *and* JEAN PERRY (ASCAP)

Out in the moon - light, here un - der the tree,

peace - ful and quiet; it's good to be me.

Here in the swamp, this is where I be - long.

14

Here with my friends, the stars, and a song.

21 Sing now a soft ser - e - nade.

25 Night - time has come to the wood and the glade.

29 Sing soft a swamp ser - e - nade.

As song ends, Frog falls asleep. During applause, lights come up as morning dawns. There is the sharp sound of a woodblock as Frog awakens and reacts to an acorn falling on his head.

FROG: Ow! *(rubs his head and looks up)*

FROGGIE: *(startled, wakes up)* What's wrong?

FROGGER: *(wakes up)* What happened?

FROG: Something thwacked me on the head.

FROGGIE:	Where? *(examines Frog's head)*
FROGGER:	Here? *(rubs Frog's head)*
FROG:	Ouch! That hurts! *(recoils)*
FROGGIE:	Something definitely hit you.
FROGGER:	*(looking around)* Where'd it come from?
FROG:	I dunno. *(points up)* Somewhere up there.
FROGGIE:	Up there?
FROGGER:	How hard did it hit?
FROG:	Pretty hard. It really hurts.
FROGGIE:	*(thoughtfully)* I'll bet it came from the sky …
FROGGER:	*(big eyes; says slowly)* Or was part of da sky …
FROG:	You mean … *(looks up)* … the … sky …
FROGGIE:	… is … *(looks up)*
FROGGER:	*(looks up)* … falling? *(The three frogs cluster together and shudder.)*

Tinker enters SL, whistling.

FROG:	Uh, excuse me sir … sir. *(Tinker looks around)* Sir … down here. *(Tinker looks down at the frogs and is obviously surprised.)*
TINKER:	Whoa! Did I hear right? Did you talk?
FROG:	That's right, and we need to tell you something.
FROGGIE:	The sky is falling. *(to Frogger)* Tell him.
FROGGER:	It's true. Da sky is falling. *(motions to Frog)*
FROG:	It thwacked me on the head and it hurt.
FROGGIE:	Show him the bump. *(Frog leans forward toward Tinker.)*
TINKER:	I don't see any bump. I see a few warts, which is normal for a frog. But … Wait a minute! I'm talking to a frog. What am I doing talking to a frog?
FROGGER:	Here. *(takes Tinker's hand and rubs it on Frog's head)* Feel dat? *(Tinker nods)*
FROG:	Ouch! Not so hard! I'm getting a headache.
TINKER:	I can't believe it. I'm carrying on a conversation with three frogs and they tell me the sky is falling. This is terrible.

FROG: It's true.

FROGGIE: It's really true.

FROGGER: True.

3a. IT'S FALLING
Frog, Froggie, Frogger, Tinker

By
DAVE *and* **JEAN PERRY** (ASCAP)

Continuing the Tradition of Shawnee Press Excellence

20

TINKER:	*(looking up)* We've got to tell everyone in the village. *(starts off SL: frogs look at each other)* Come on! *(turns back, sees that the frogs haven't moved, motions for them to follow)* Hop to it! *(frogs all take one hop toward him and hurry to catch up as they follow him off SL)*
FROG:	Wait a moment. *(tilts his head to listen)* Someone's coming.
FROGGIE:	What will we do?
FROGGER:	Just hold very still. *(Frogs freeze. Tinker looks SL to see.)*
TINKER:	It looks like three maids. I'll talk to them. *(Three maids enter SL; Tinker bows.)* Greetings.
ALEXIS:	Hello.
DENISE:	It's a pleasant morning.
PRISCILLA:	We can't stay to talk. We're on our way to the village to sell our cheese …
ALEXIS:	… and milk …
DENISE:	and eggs.
PRISCILLA:	Yes, there's a fair at the school …
ALEXIS:	And there will be games and prizes …
DENISE:	And they're even going to have a hop!
FROG:	*(to the other frogs, out of the side of his mouth so that the maids won't hear him)* Hey, did you hear that? A hop!
FROGGIE:	*(leaning toward the frogs and trying not to be noticed)* Yeah, it sounds like fun!
FROGGER:	*(also remaining frozen in place)* Hey, dat's what I do … Hop!
TINKER:	Oh. May we join you?
PRISCILLA:	We?
TINKER:	Yes, we're also going to the village.
ALEXIS:	What do you mean, "we"?
TINKER:	Oh, the frogs … and … me.
DENISE:	Oh, you're taking the frogs to the village to sell? Fried frog legs make a delicious meal. *(frogs shudder)*
TINKER:	Well, actually, we need to warn the village that the sky is falling and part of it fell on <u>his</u> head. *(motions to Frog.)*

PRISCILLA: Wait a minute! Did you say the sky is falling?

FROG: Or cracked or something. It thwacked me on the head.

FROGGIE: There's a bump right here. (*pushes Frog's head down and points to the bump*)

FROGGER: Ya wanna feel da bump? Gimme your hand. (*reaches for Alexis' hand which she quickly jerks away*)

ALEXIS: Ooo … warts.

DENISE: (*in shock, pointing at frogs and backing away*) I … frogs … talking …

PRISCILLA: Wait a minute! Hold the phone! Are these frogs …?

TINKER: Talking. Yes. It's somewhat unusual, but in light of the imminent danger, I don't think we should let these eccentricities bother us.

ALEXIS: Do you <u>really</u> think the sky is falling?

FROG: Sure do. A piece of it thwacked me right on the old bean.

TINKER: Come on, let's go!

3b. IT'S FALLING

Frog, Froggie, Frogger, Tinker, and Maids

By
DAVE *and* JEAN PERRY (ASCAP)

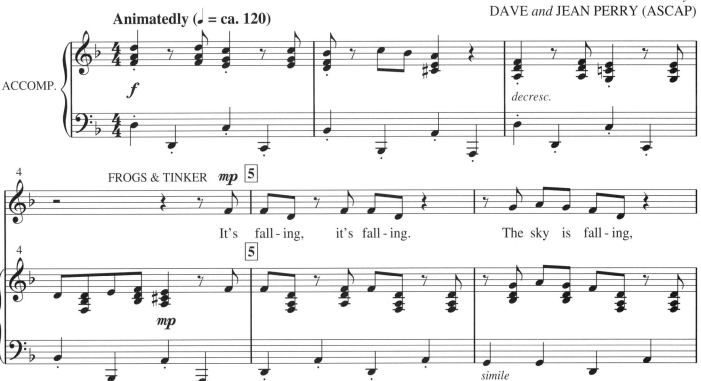

Continuing the Tradition of Shawnee Press Excellence

Frogs, Maids, and Tinker exit SR. Narrators enter SL.

NARRATOR 1:   And so …

NARRATOR 2:   *(interrupts)* I've been thinking about that frog when the sky hit him on the head.

NARRATOR 1:   … and …?

NARRATOR 2:   I'll bet he almost croaked! *(laughs at his own joke)*

NARRATOR 1:   *(annoyed)* And so the frogs, Tinker, and the three maids soon arrived at the school where the festival was in full swing.

Music begins. Narrators exit SL, curtains open and lights come up to reveal the school where the Hop is taking place.

4. THE HOP
Students, Townspeople, Teachers, Frogs, Maids, and Tinker

By
DAVE *and* JEAN PERRY (ASCAP)

Continuing the Tradition of Shawnee Press Excellence

28

30

do the chick-en flap and shuf-fle a-round__ with our feet.

spoken **mf** 57

Now, get down low__ and hop like a big green frog.

mf

All freeze and roll eyes, looking for a fly.

Now, sit real still__ like you're sit-tin'__ on a log.

Using hand or tongue, catch and swallow fly with a big gulp. 65

Hop a-round some more.__

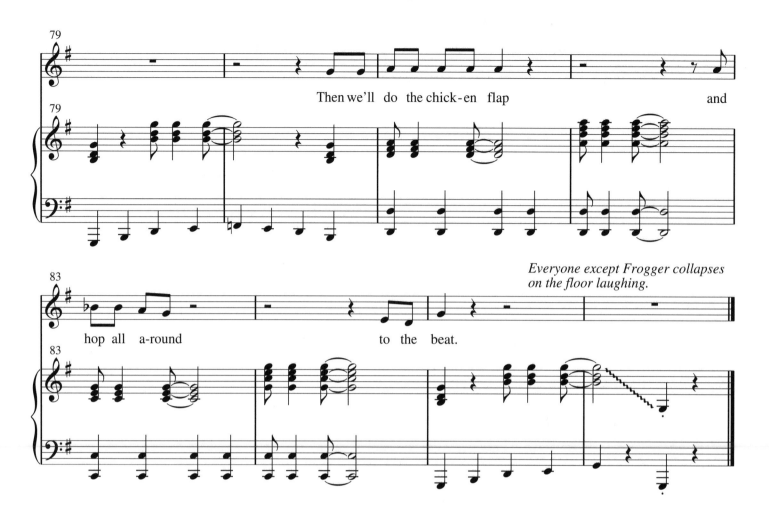

FROGGER:	*(bellowing)* Hey, everybody! *(Everyone freezes and the room becomes silent.)* I want your undivided attention. Somethin' very unusual is happenin'.
ED:	*(from the back)* Yeah, a frog's talking.

Everyone reacts with a lively discussion including: "A frog's talking." "I've never heard of a talking frog." "Is he really talking?" "There are three of them." "Do they all talk?" "Don't get too close. Warts!"

FROGGER:	Hey! *(Everyone freezes and is silent.)* I believe dat I asked you for your undivided attention.
TINKER:	Maybe I should talk. *(steps forward)* What my friend Frogger is trying to say is that the sky is falling.
CHORUS:	*(slowly looking up)* What?
FROGGIE:	It's true. He's got a bump on his head to prove it.
FROGGER:	Ya wanna feel it? Here. *(reaches for chorus member's hand)*

FROG:	Please … no … not again. *(Winces as several hands reach out to feel the bump on his head.)*
BECKA:	That's a dandy.
EMILY:	I'll bet it hurts.
FROG:	Ow.
MIKE:	That's nothin'. You should have seen the egg that I got when …
RACHEL:	*(to Frog)* Are you sure you're a frog? I remember reading about a Prince …
TINKER:	*(interrupting)* The point is … the sky is falling and we've got to do something! Is there anyone here who can help us?
MISS FINKLETON:	*(steps forward, carrying a stack of books)* Excuse me, I am the librarian and I will be happy to research the situation, but I must have quiet.
CHORUS:	*(everyone tiptoes and begins whispering ad lib.)* What will she do? Do you think she has a plan? This is terrible. I hope she can tell us what to do, *etc.*
MISS FINKLETON:	I SAID … quiet. *(hands the stack of books to Tinker; selects one of the books and begins paging through it)* Now, let's see … sky … falling. Would that fall under current events, self-improvement, sci … *(realizes she said something funny)* Oh dear. I believe I've made a pun. Would "the sky is falling" FALL under … Oh, that is funny.
RACHEL:	But it doesn't seem logical that … what I mean is … I think we need to analyze the problem in a precise and orderly fashion. We need to go where the sky fell and once we have all the information …
COACH KLAXTON:	*(pushes forward, chewing gum)* Hi. We got a problem here? If we work as a team, there's no hurdle that we can't overcome, no barrier we can't cross, no obstacle too big for us. But we have to hustle! We have to get out there and fight! We can win! We can do it! Hands in the center!

Miss Finkleton, Becka, and Mike put their hands on top of Klaxton's extended right hand. As the music begins, a frustrated Rachel steps to the side, crosses her arms and watches in disbelief.

COACH KLAXTON, MISS FINKLETON, BECKA, MIKE:	Go … Go … Go … GO!!

5a. WE'RE GONNA WIN!

Coach Klaxton, Miss Finkleton, Students, Townspeople, Tinker, Maids, and Frogs

By
DAVE *and* JEAN PERRY (ASCAP)

Continuing the Tradition of Shawnee Press Excellence

Chorus splits, breaks into a march, imitating a band.

ta, ta ta ta, ta ta ta ta ta ta ta.

COACH KLAXTON

Out of the hud - dle now,

show some piz - zazz__ and wow, do what you must do. __

MISS FINKLETON

There is no stop - ping us, no wor - ry, strain__ or fuss. We are com - ing through.

Shoul-der to shoul - der, we're stand -ing tall,___ and

now it's time to be - gin.___ Chin up and show_ your pride;

come on and hit___ your stride. We are gon - na win!

simile

COACH KLAXTON:	So, what do you say? How about a little hustle and teamwork? Let's get warmed up, run a few sprints, and then get out there and …
RACHEL:	… and what?
COACH KLAXTON:	We'll get out there and we'll fight and win and … and…
RACHEL:	<u>What</u> will we fight? Until we have thoroughly analyzed the problem we won't know what we're up against.
COACH KLAXTON:	But we can't sit around and wait for the sky to bonk someone else on the noggin.
EMILY:	We need some leadership.
RACHEL:	Some guidance.
BECKA:	Someone with wisdom. *(Coach Klaxton edges forward.)*
ED:	Someone we all respect.
EMILY:	Someone who can make the tough decisions.
COACH KLAXTON:	*(steps forward)* And … here … I …
BECKA:	Excuse me, I think we need *(thoughtfully looks around)* … the Mayor!
COACH KLAXTON:	(brushes her aside) Nonsense, I can do …
ED:	*(pushing forward)* She's right. We need the Mayor.
MIKE:	I'll go get him! *(hurries off SL)*
COACH KLAXTON:	But I can handle this.
BECKA:	No! We need the Mayor. *(turns to the cast and leads them in chanting)*
CAST:	WE NEED THE MAYOR! WE NEED THE MAYOR! WE NEED THE MAYOR!

5b. HE WILL SAVE THE DAY!*

Students, Townspeople, Teachers, Tinker, Maids, and Frogs

By
DAVE *and* JEAN PERRY (ASCAP)

* If Mayor is played by a girl, change to "she" throughout.

Continuing the Tradition of Shawnee Press Excellence

THWACKED – Teacher Edition

save the day!

After the song, everyone applauds the arrival of the Mayor and Council Members.

MAYOR:	Calm down! Calm down, everyone! Now what's this I hear about a spy calling?
MISS FINKLETON:	It's the sky. The <u>sky</u> … <u>is</u> … <u>falling</u>!
COACH KLAXTON:	I was just getting everyone organized with a lot of teamwork and a pep talk and …
MAYOR:	*(to Miss Finkleton)* Where did you hear about this?
MISS FINKLETON:	From a reliable source.
MAYOR:	And what is this reliable source?
RACHEL:	A frog.
MAYOR:	A frog! *(starts laughing)*
RACHEL:	That's right and, although I haven't had time to run any tests, I …
MAYOR:	*(interrupting)* You heard from a frog that the sky is falling? Are you nutty?
CAST:	*(reacts, ad lib.)* Well … I don't believe I am. Nope … feel just fine. I don't believe so. Uh … nooo. Thanks for asking, but no. Most certainly not! *(etc.)*
FROG:	*(pushes his way forward to the Mayor)* Excuse me, Mr. Mayor, it's true.
MAYOR:	*(looks down at Frog)* What?
FROG:	The sky is falling.
RACHEL:	Mr. Mayor, I just don't see how it's possible …
MAYOR:	*(to Frog, ignoring Rachel)* And … just how do you know that it's falling?
FROG:	It thwacked me on the head.

MAYOR:	Where did this … ? Wait a minute. Am I talking to a fro … ? I'm talking to a frog! My career is ruined. Once the media gets hold of this, I'll be in all the tabloids: "Mayor Has Conversation with Frog."
FROGGIE:	*(moves forward)* But it's true. The sky is falling and he's got a bump on his head to prove it.
FROG:	Not this again.
FROGGER:	*(has moved forward to address the Mayor)* Wanna feel da bump? *(reaches for Mayor's hand)*
MAYOR:	*(pulling his hand away)* Warts!
THREE FROGS:	Warts?
MAYOR:	Look … I shake hands, I kiss babies, but I don't do frogs.
FROGGER:	O.K., but trust me, dere's a bump on his cabeza from a piece of duh sky dat fell.
CAST:	*(all speaking at once, ad lib.)* It's there alright. Sure is. I felt it. It's big. Right on top of his noodle. *(etc.)*
ED:	*(to Mayor)* We've got to do something!
BECKA:	Please, Mr. Mayor, tell us what to do!
EMILY:	This is terrible!
CAST:	*(all speaking at once, ad lib.)* This is an emergency. You've got to help us. What should we do? *(etc.)*
MAYOR:	*(raising his hands to quiet the crowd)* Ahem. If I could have your attention. *(crowd continues talking)* Please! Quiet down!

Coach Klaxton blows his whistle. Crowd stops talking.

COACH KLAXTON:	O.K., team, settle down. *(looks at the Mayor)*
MIKE:	What's the plan?
BECKA:	Tell us what to do.
RACHEL:	*(pleading)* But, Mr. Mayor …
MAYOR:	*(addressing the crowd)* Ahem … yes … well … as I was going to say. *(chorus does a big inhale of breath)* I don't have a plan, *(chorus does a big exhale)* but … I am working on one.
EMILY:	But YOU are the Mayor.
MAYOR:	That's right! I must make a wise decision and that takes time. I need to confer with the town council.
ED:	But … the sky is falling!

6a. IT WOULDN'T BE WISE

Mayor, Council, Students, Townspeople, Teachers, Tinker, Maids, and Frogs

By
DAVE *and* JEAN PERRY (ASCAP)

Continuing the Tradition of Shawnee Press Excellence

THWACKED – Teacher Edition

After the song, the Mayor summons the Council Members DSL to discuss the situation.

COUNCIL MEMBER #1: So what do we do now?

RACHEL: *(pushes forward)* I have an idea.

COUNCIL MEMBER #2: *(ignores her)* I say we run!

COUNCIL MEMBER #3: That's a good idea. Let's go!

COUNCIL MEMBER #4: Hmm …

COUNCIL MEMBER #1: Where?

COUNCIL MEMBER #2: What do you mean?

COUNCIL MEMBER #1: Where do we run to?

RACHEL: *(pushes forward again)* It's really a <u>good</u> idea!

COUNCIL MEMBER #2: *(steps in front of Rachel)* Er … well … Maybe we should hide?

COUNCIL MEMBER #3: That's a good idea. Let's go!

COUNCIL MEMBER #4: Hmm …

COUNCIL MEMBER #1: Where?

COUNCIL MEMBER #2: Uh … right here in the school.

RACHEL: *(pushes forward)* I think we should go see where the sky fell!

COUNCIL MEMBER #1: *(ignores her)* What if the falling sky knocks a hole in the roof?

COUNCIL MEMBER #2: Well, then, I suppose … Look, would you stop asking so many questions!

MAYOR: *(steps forward)* Perhaps we should go see where the sky fell.

RACHEL: *(frustrated)* I just said that.

COUNCIL MEMBER #1: Are you sure?

COUNCIL MEMBER #2: We need more information.

COUNCIL MEMBER #3: That's a good idea. Let's go!

COUNCIL MEMBER #4: Hmm …

Everyone follows the Mayor and the Council as they leave the stage and walk into the audience, eventually arriving at the tree and the swamp. As the music continues, Narrators enter SL.

6b. IT WOULDN'T BE WISE
Instrumental

By
DAVE *and* JEAN PERRY (ASCAP)

Continuing the Tradition of Shawnee Press Excellence

NARRATOR 1: Off they went, the entire town, back to the swamp to see where the sky fell.

NARRATOR 2: They were a merry lot as they hurried along; skipping, running, playing leapfrog.

NARRATOR 1: *(very annoyed)* Please ... no more frog jokes! *(regains composure ...to audience)*
As they reached the marsh ....

NARRATOR 2: They were swamped with ideas.

NARRATOR 1: *(ignoring Narrator 2)* They began to look for where the sky had fallen.

NARRATOR 2: Ribbit. Rib ... *(Narrator 1 clamps his hand over Narrator 2's mouth and pulls him off SL.)*

Everyone arrives at the swamp SR, stops and looks around in wonder at the surroundings.

COACH KLAXTON: *(dismayed)* This is it?

MISS FINKLETON: *(looking around)* This is where the sky fell?

RACHEL: *(looking up and squinting)* Interesting. It looks O.K. to me.

COUNCIL MEMBER #2:   *(steps forward in front of Rachel)* Excuse me. You're in the way.

COUNCIL MEMBER #4:   *(to Frog)* Where exactly were you when the sky fell?

FROG: It was a <u>piece</u> of the sky that fell and *(points to the log SR)* I was sitting over there.

RACHEL: *(moving forward next to Council Member #2)* How could the sky fall?

COUNCIL MEMBER #2:   *(pushing Rachel to the side)* Would you <u>please</u> move!

RACHEL: *(to Frog)* Go to where you were sitting.

COUNCIL MEMBER #4:   Walk softly. The sky is obviously weak in this area and more of it could fall at any time.

MAYOR: We should all stay back. I don't want anyone getting hurt.

RACHEL: It looks fine to me.

COACH KLAXTON: O.K., team, move back. You too, girlie. Give them some room.

MISS FINKLETON: And keep quiet. Shh!

Frog sits on the log that he was sitting on at the beginning of the story. Council members gather around to study the situation.

FROG: This is where I was sitting.

COUNCIL MEMBER #1:   Hmm …

COUNCIL MEMBER #2:   Hmm …

COUNCIL MEMBER #3:   Hmm …

RACHEL: *(examines notes)* It just doesn't make sense …

COUNCIL MEMBER #4:   *(annoyed)* Excuse me. *(pause)* Hmm …

MAYOR: *(to council members)* Are you thinking … ?

COUNCIL MEMBERS: *(nodding)* Mmm … hmm.

56

RACHEL:	*(looks up from notes)* But this is silly! There's nothing wrong with the sky.
MISS FINKLETON:	*(leans forward and places her hand on Rachel's shoulder)* Quiet! Please. Shh.
FROGGIE:	Well, something hit him on the head!
FROGGER:	And he's got da bump to prove it. Wanna feel? *(starts toward Frog)*
FROG:	No touch! *(He takes up a karate stance and slowly looks around waiting for anyone to move toward him … everyone takes a step back, except for Rachel.)*
RACHEL:	*(exasperated)* Look, there's nothing wrong with the sky. Why won't you listen to me?
MAYOR:	This is an adult matter. Please, Miss Finkleton, remove this child.

Rachel breaks away from Miss Finkleton's grasp and crosses SL. As the music begins, the cast steps back and freezes as Rachel steps forward.

7. BELIEVE IN YOURSELF
Rachel and Cast

By
DAVE *and* JEAN PERRY (ASCAP)

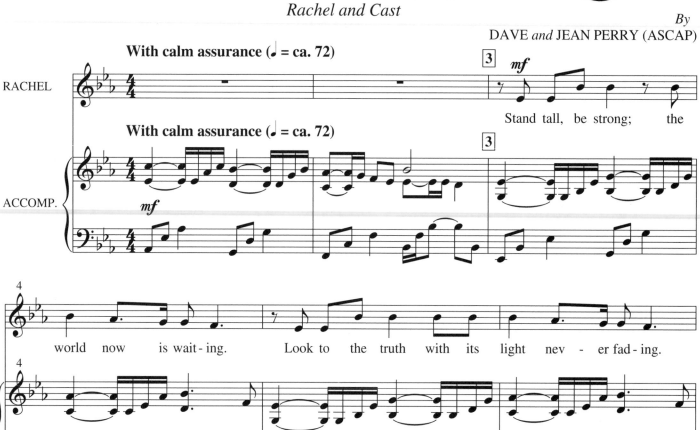

Continuing the Tradition of Shawnee Press Excellence

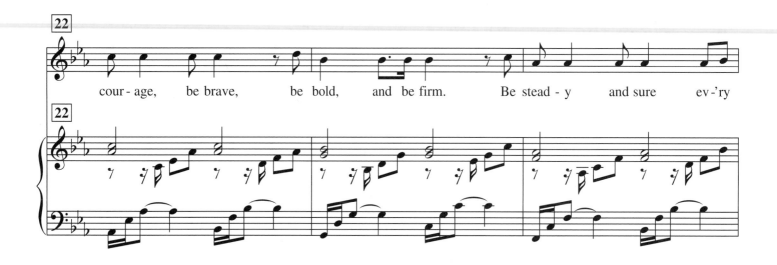

day.   Trust   in your-self.   Be-lieve   in your-self.   Hold

CAST

Ah _____   *ah* _____

true   to your-self,   al - ways.   Stand tall, be strong,   the

ah _____

world   now   is wait-ing.   Look to   the truth with its   light   nev - er fad-ing.

cresc.

Reach for the stars, let them guide and in-spire you. Stand tall, be sure, be

At cutoff, Rachel whirls around to see who is singing, but the cast remains frozen.

strong.   Stand tall, be sure,   be strong!_____

CAST

Ah_____

After the song, Rachel walks back to Frog and looks around. She stops when she sees an acorn on the ground.

RACHEL: That's it! *(She picks an acorn off the ground near Frog, lifts it up and drops it on Frog's head.)*

FROG: Ouch! Right on my sore spot. What'd you do that for?

RACHEL: What did that feel like?

FROG: Like the sky is fall … Like an acorn hit me on the head!

RACHEL:	Yes! At last we have the facts:

           A. No one else has been hit on the head.
           B. The sky looks perfectly perfect.
           C. Frog was sitting under an oak tree, and
           D. There is an acorn on the ground nearby.
So what are we to deduce from this?

CAST: *(all speaking at once, ad lib.)* Not falling? Is it true? That's what he said. I wondered about this! Can you believe they thought the sky was falling? Just goes to show, you can't take the word of a frog! *(etc.)*

COACH KLAXTON: That's it, team. Let's move along. Nothing to see here.

ED: Well, what about the frog?

COUNCIL MEMBER #1: He's the one who came up with this crazy story. *(Froggie and Frogger begin moving away from Frog)*

COUNCIL MEMBER #2: Yeah.

COUNCIL MEMBER #3: *(moving menacingly toward Frog)* Yeah!

RACHEL: *(stands in front of Frog, fists clenched, ready to do battle)* Hold it, Mister! No one touches the frog! It's not his fault that he was thwacked on the noodle with an acorn.

FROG: It's still sore.

RACHEL: And … none of you even questioned his story!

Mayor, Council Members, and the rest of the cast (including Froggie and Frogger) hang their heads and mumble words of apology.

RACHEL: After all, it was just an honest mistake made by an innocent creature who just happens to be green … and slimy … and has warts … *(Frog interrupts)*

FROG: Thank you for those kind words. *(to everyone)* I would like to apologize for the inconvenience that I have caused all of you. I honestly thought that the sky was falling. And I do have a sore head.

RACHEL: Here, this will make it better. *(She leans forward and kisses Frog on the top of his head, then wipes her mouth.)* Yuck!!!

The lights flicker and go out. There is a lot of commotion and talking among the cast: "What happened? "What's going on?" "Did the sun go out?" "Help!" [etc.] During the commotion, while the lights are out, the boy playing Frog exits the stage and the boy playing the Prince takes his position.

PRINCE: *(his voice changes to a normal boy's voice as he speaks)* Whoa! What's happening? This is weird.

Lights come up to reveal the Prince standing where Frog had been. Prince is rubbing the bump on his head as he looks in wonder at his royal clothes.

RACHEL: Who are you? Where's the frog? I've never seen you before. What did you do with the frog? If you've hurt him …

PRINCE: *(looks at his hands as he flexes his fingers)* Does anyone have a mirror? *(He lifts one foot and inspects it as he wiggles his ankle.)*

TINKER: I have one. *(hands the mirror to the Prince)* Here.

PRINCE: Thanks. *(inspects his face and profile in the mirror)* Not bad. Warts are gone; chin is back; pearlies look good. *(looks at audience)* I think the spell is broken!

RACHEL: *(tugging at the Prince's sleeve)* I want to know …

PRINCE: *(turns, looks at the girl and smiles)* Yes? What would you like to know?

RACHEL: *(taken aback at the sight of this good-looking prince.)* Have you … seen … a frog?

PRINCE: Why yes, I am that frog, but now I'm not. I'm … ME!

RACHEL: It's starting to all make sense.

Council members each lean forward as they speak.

COUNCIL MEMBER #1:   But ….

COUNCIL MEMBER #2:   … who ….

COUNCIL MEMBER #3:   … are …

COUNCIL MEMBER #4:   you?

PRINCE: I'm a bit Froggy … er … I mean, foggy on that but it's all starting to come back. Let's see … I used to be a Prince …

RACHEL: So, you lived in a castle.

PRINCE: Then I was rude to an old lady …

RACHEL: … and … I'll bet she turned you into a frog! *(music begins)*

PRINCE: Yes, and I hopped down to the swamp and ate flies and … *(singing begins)*

8. AMAZING!
Entire Cast

By
DAVE *and* **JEAN PERRY** (ASCAP)

Continuing the Tradition of Shawnee Press Excellence

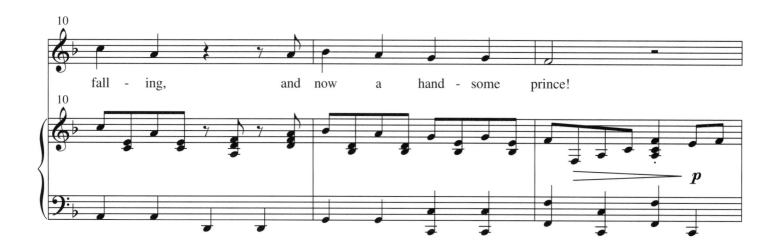

fall - ing, and now a hand - some prince!

NARRATOR 1: That's the story. The sky never fell. The village and swamp returned to normal, and the Prince returned

to his home in the castle. His experience as a frog had changed him into a humble and agreeable young man.

NARRATOR 2: He remained friends with the villagers and consulted frequently with his best friend, Rachel.

NARRATOR 1: Every now and then, he would join his frog friends for a relaxed evening of singing ...

NARRATOR 2: ... and dining in the swamp.

NARRATOR 1: Oddly enough, he still had an occasional yearning for flies.

NARRATOR 2: Ribbit.

(Divide Chorus evenly on parts)

This is a - maz - ing! This is stu - pen - dous! What a

This is a - maz - ing! This is stu - pen - dous! What a

THWACKED – Teacher Edition

9. EXIT MUSIC
Instrumental

By
DAVE *and* JEAN PERRY (ASCAP)

Continuing the Tradition of Shawnee Press Excellence

THWACKED – Teacher Edition

Dave and Jean Perry have been writing and publishing songs for schools and churches for over thirty years. Dave's twenty-eight years as a high school choral director and Jean's twenty-five years as a middle school/elementary choral/general music teacher give them a unique view of what is needed for today's young singers. Dave and Jean have composed, edited and arranged various songs for the recital hall or festival with the young singer in mind.

Dave is a recipient of the "Excellence in Teaching" award from the Arizona Music Educators Association. In the year 2000, he was selected as the "Arizona Music Educator of the Year" and also received the "Lifetime Recognition Award" from the Choral Directors of Arizona.

Jean has received the "Excellence in Teaching" award from the Arizona Music Educators Association, the "Teacher of the Month" award from Mesa Public Schools, the "Outstanding Choral Educator Award" (2001) from the Arizona chapter of the American Choral Directors Association and the "Arizona Music Educator of the Year" (2002).

In 2009, Dave and Jean were selected to receive the William E. Richardson Retired Music Educator Service Award from the Arizona Music Educators Association.

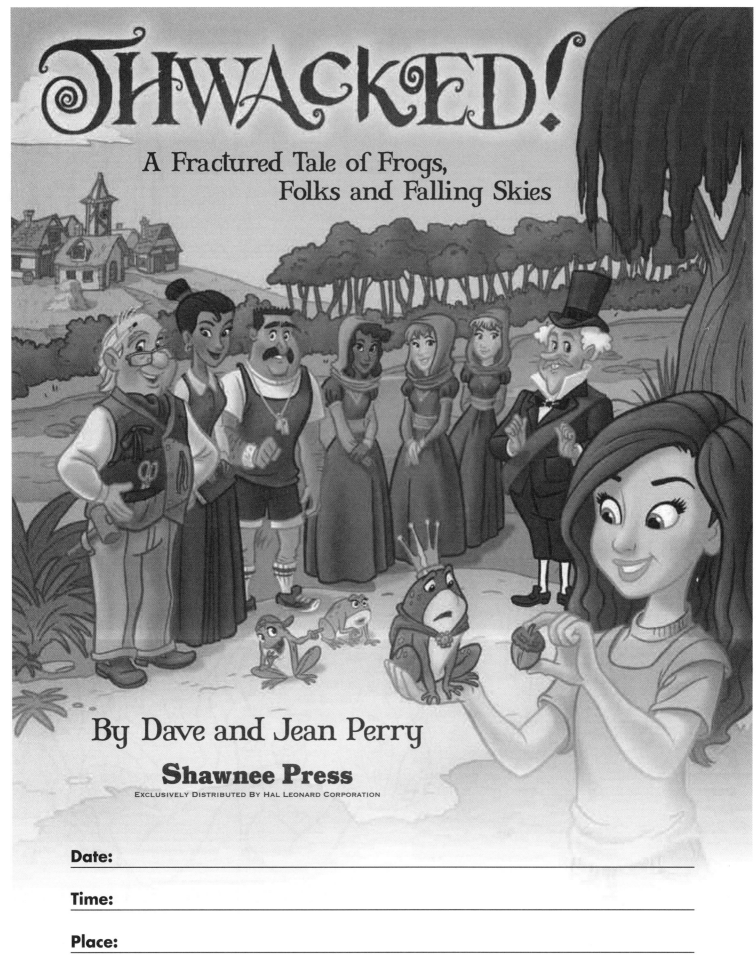

THWACKED!

A Fractured Tale of Frogs, Folks and Falling Skies

By Dave and Jean Perry

Shawnee Press

EXCLUSIVELY DISTRIBUTED BY HAL LEONARD CORPORATION

Date: _____

Time: _____

Place: _____